In this book, you will need:

Paint
Poster paints or acrylic paints are best for these projects.

Paintbrushes
It's good to have a few different-sized paintbrushes. Remember to always clean your paintbrush after you've finished your craft.

Coloured card or paper
To make your pictures and crafts with. You don't have to use the colours suggested in this book.

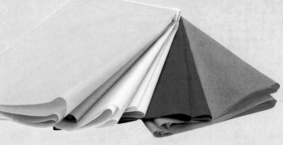

Glue
PVA is great for mixing into paint to make it stronger. Glue sticks are useful for sticking pictures to card to make frames.

Scissors
Use child-size scissors. Ask an adult to help you with any tricky bits.

Mixing palette
To hold the paint and to mix different colours

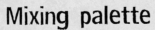

Colour Wheel

You will need:
Thin card
Compass
Pencil
Scissors
Ruler
Red, blue and yellow paint
Paintbrush
Mixing palette

You can have lots of fun with paint, but do you know what colours go well with others? Make this handy wheel to help you make great colour choices and learn how to mix colours.

1 Draw a large circle on the card with your compass. Cut out the circle.

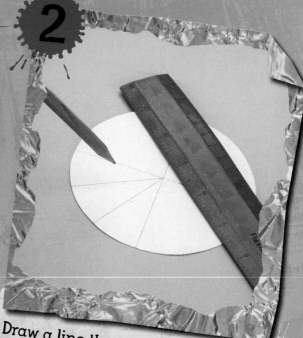

2 Draw a line through the middle and then across to create 4 equal quarters. Divide each quarter into three to make twelve sections.

Contents

Fun with Paint

You can have lots of fun with paint. In this book, you can paint with your fingers, with cotton buds and with scrunched up paper. You can even add different textures to the paint such as rice or oats.

You can also mix paints. Did you know that with just three colours, red, blue and yellow, you can mix together a whole range of colours? These are called the three primary colours and by mixing them in different combinations, you can make any colour you want!

Before you start painting, always cover surfaces with newspaper so it's easy to clear up any spills. Put on an apron or an old top. Find a space where you can leave your projects to dry. Then you're ready to paint!

Fun with Print

Clever Crafts for Little Fingers

Annalees Lim

Published in paperback in 2014 by Wayland
Copyright © Wayland 2014

Wayland
Hachette Children's Books
338 Euston Road
London NW1 3BR

Wayland Australia
Level 17/207 Kent Street
Sydney NSW 2000

Editor: Victoria Brooker
Designer: Lisa Peacock
Step-by-step photographs: Simon Pask, N1 Studios
Images used for creative graphics: Shutterstock
Cover picture: Thanks to Evelyn Burke

British Library Cataloguing in Publication Data

Lim, Annalees.
  Fun with paint. -- (Clever crafts for little fingers)
  1. Painting--Juvenile literature.
  I. Title II. Series
  751.4-dc23

ISBN: 978 0 7502 8078 5

Printed in China

10 9 8 7 6 5 4 3 2 1

Wayland is a division of Hachette Children's Books,
an Hachette UK Company.
www.hachette.co.uk

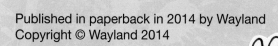

For templates and more craft tips and
activities, go to:
www.wayland.co.uk/downloads

3

Paint a primary colour (red, blue and yellow) in each third of the circle, making sure there are three blank sections between each one.

4

Paint your secondary colours (purple, orange and green) next. For purple, mix blue and red. For orange, mix red and yellow. For green, mix yellow and blue.

Colours directly opposite each other on the colour wheel are contrasting colours. This means they go well with each other. Colours that are beside each other on the colour wheel are complimentary colours and work in harmony with each other.

5

For the tertiary colours, mix whatever colours are either side of the blank section you want to fill. For example, mix primary yellow and secondary green to make light green.

Handy Farmyard

Create a whole farmyard full of animals just by using your hands. First learn to print a whole herd of clucking chickens, and when you get the hang of it there are lots more animals you can try your hand at!

Fill your farmyard: Try printing a cow with horns and hoofs; a peacock with long feathers; a sitting duck with a beak and wings; or a sheep with a fluffy coat and tail.

You will need:
Paint
Paintbrush
White paper
Coloured paper
Pen
Glue

1

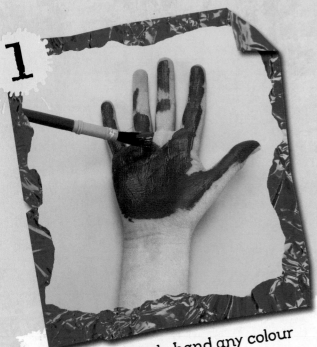

Paint you whole hand any colour you like.

2

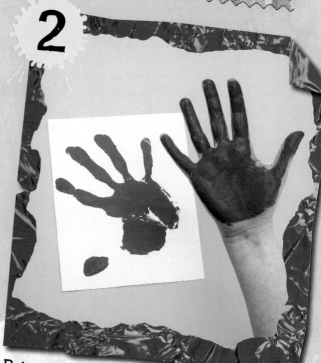

Print your hand onto a white piece of paper and leave to dry.

3

Use a black pen to draw the outline of your chicken, using the handprint as a guide. Start drawing a head with a beak and wattle on the thumb.

4

Cut out your handprint chicken and glue it to a coloured background. Try a green piece of paper to look like grass. Now try a different animal!

Wax Crayon Batik Owl

You will need:
A pale coloured crayon
White paper
Watered-down paint or
  watercolours
Cotton bud
Coloured paper
Scissors
Glue

Batik was used by the ancient Egyptians. You can have a go too, with this simple method using just your wax crayons and some watery paint.

Mix some watery paints in your palette. Paint over the whole page. Use different shades and blend them with water.

Draw a picture of an owl with your crayon. You could copy the one above or copy one from a book.

Use the same technique to send secret notes to friends. Write your note in crayon and ask your friend to paint over to reveal what you've said!

3

Before the paint completely dries use the cotton bud to wipe off the paint from the wax crayon lines. This will make the lines really bright.

4

Make a frame for your picture by folding a piece of card in half and cutting out the middle. Make the sides uneven to make it look like the owl is poking out through leaves.

5

Glue the frame on top of your owl. Your owl picture is now ready to hang in your bedroom!

Dotty About Fireworks

You will need:
Paint
Black paper or card
Cotton buds
Grey paper or card
Scissors
Pencil
Ruler
Glue

Watch fireworks whizzing and banging in a starry sky all year round by painting your own scene. You could make them really sparkle and shimmer by sprinkling the wet paint with glitter.

1 Paint a red firework in the middle of the black card using a cotton bud to make the dots.

2 Paint two more fireworks in different colours either side using the same technique.

3

Paint bright yellow bursts of dots in the centre of each firework and white dots on the outside. Leave to dry.

4

Draw a skyline onto the grey paper and cut out.

5

Glue the skyline onto the bottom of the black card. Your picture is ready to display!

Scrunched Seascape

You will need:

White paper
Paint
Scrunched-up newspaper
  or tissue paper
Scissors
Glue

Painting waves and sunny skies can take a while to learn, but with this simple technique you can create a fantastic seascape that will make you look like a master painter!

All sorts of shapes can be cut out of the stippled paper to create a different scene.

1

Scrunch up old bits of tissue paper into small balls.

2

Dunk the balls in paint and stamp them lightly all over a blank piece of paper. Make lots of sheets using different colours of paint.

3

Once the paper is dry, cut into shapes that will make your seascape. You will need some waves, a beach, a sun and a palm tree.

4

Stick your shapes onto a blue painted background. Try making different scenes using this technique.

Snowflake Wrapping Paper

Stencils are a quick and easy way to make repeat patterns and add a bit of colour to any plain bits of paper. The stencils are also really fun to make and, just like real snowflakes, they come out differently each time!

You will need:
Paper
Scissors
Paint
Paintbrush

1

Fold a piece of paper in half, then quarters and then fold in half again to make a triangle shape.

2

Trim the top so it looks like an ice cream cone in shape.

3

Cut shapes into the cone shape. Open it up to reveal your snowflake stencil.

You could make the wrapping paper extra special by dabbing glue on and then sprinkling glitter on top.

4

Place the snowflake on a large piece of paper and dab paint through the holes of the stencil. Cover your whole piece of paper with snowflakes.

3-D Rainbow

Mix together this gloopy paint recipe to create a beautiful rainbow that really stands out from the page.

You will need:

Mixing pot
Paint
PVA glue
Porridge oats, rice, sugar or pencil sharpenings
Compass
Pencil
Paper
Shiny or sparkly paper

1

In a pot, mix 1 part glue to 3 parts paint. Add your chosen texture (oats, rice, sugar or sharpenings) and mix well. Make four of these mixtures in different colours.

2

Using a compass, draw a semi-circle to make the shape of a rainbow.

Try using the same technique to create wavy waves in a seascape or give people funky hairstyles on top of faces you have painted.

3

Paint a thick line of textured paint onto the semi-circle. Paint another line underneath and so on to create your rainbow.

4

Cut out shiny clouds and rain and glue on to the picture to make your scene complete.

River Reflections

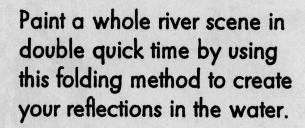

You will need:
Pale blue paper
Paintbrush
Paint

Paint a whole river scene in double quick time by using this folding method to create your reflections in the water.

1 Fold a piece of pale blue paper in half, long ways.

2 Paint the bottom half in a darker shade of blue. Use watery paint so that it looks more like a river.

You can print other reflections too. Try palm trees in a desert oasis or tall city buildings that are beside a wide river.

3

Paint a landscape on the top half of the paper full of trees, bushes and flowers.

4

Fold the paper in half and press firmly. Open up carefully to reveal your river reflection!

Foil Prints

You will need:
Blank cards or folded plain paper
Tin foil
Scissors
Blunt pencil
Paint
Paint brush

Tin foil that you find in your kitchen cupboards is not only useful when baking or cooking, it is a great craft material that you can use to make fantastic repeat patterns.

1

Cut a large piece of tin foil and fold it in half.

Try drawing letters of your name to make a simple bedroom sign. Just remember to write everything backwards so it prints the right way round!

2

Using a blunt pencil, draw an outline of a house. Press firmly so that it makes a deep dent. This is easier to do if you lean on a stack of magazines or paper.

3

Cover the drawing with a thin layer of paint.

4

Place the foil print on top of your blank card or folded paper and press firmly.

5

Carefully peel of the foil print. Your card print is ready to send. Try different pictures and colours.

Glossary

beak the hard part of a bird's mouth

blunt not sharp

primary colour red, yellow and blue

secondary colour a colour made by mixing two of the primary colours together

skyline the outline of buildings against sky

stencil a piece of paper or card with a picture that has been cut out through which paint or pens is drawn onto another piece of paper to make a picture

technique the particular way of doing something

tertiary colour a colour made by mixing a primary and a secondary colour together

texture the feel or look of a surface

wattle a flap of skin that hangs from the neck of a bird

Index